USBORNE SCIENCE ACTIVITIES

Rebecca Heddle and Paul Shipton

Designed by Sue Grobecker and Susie McCaffrey

Illustrated by Kate Davies

Edited by Helen Edom and Rebecca Heddle

Contents

OCT   2009

SCIENCE WITH
BATTERIES

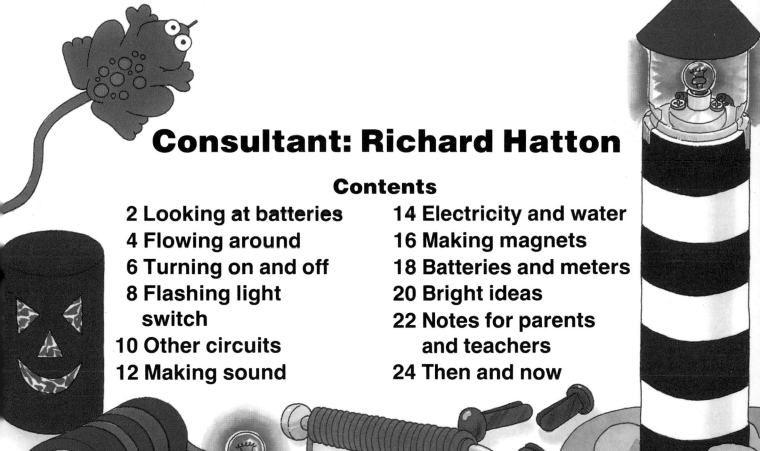

Consultant: Richard Hatton

Contents

Looking at batteries

Batteries make the electricity which works things like watches and toys. Look at the batteries in things around your house.

This radio uses four batteries.

Some watches need tiny batteries.

All batteries have a number with a V after it. The V stands for volts and the number is the battery's voltage. Batteries with a high voltage are stronger than batteries with a low voltage.

Which of your batteries has the highest voltage?

4.5V

1.5V

Light up

You need:
three 1.5 volt batteries,
2 pieces of plastic-covered wire *,
3.5 volt bulb in bulb holder *,
screwdriver,
scissors,
adhesive tape.

Ask an adult to strip about 2cm (1in) of plastic off each end of the wires.

The two metal ends of the battery are called terminals. One terminal is flat and one is button-shaped. Tape a wire to the flat terminal.

The metal wire must touch the flat terminal.

Screwdriver

Bulb

Hook the other end of the wire under a screw in the bulb holder. Screw it down with a screwdriver. Fasten the second wire under the other screw.

Bulb holder

Second wire

2

*You can buy these at an electrical shop or hardware store. Page 22 shows you which wires you can use.

Touch the free end of the second wire to the button terminal of the battery. The bulb lights because the battery pushes electricity through it.

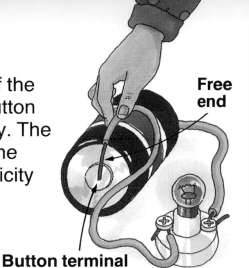

Free end

Button terminal

Tape the flat end of a second battery to the button end of the first battery. Touch the free wire to the button terminal of the second battery. What happens to the bulb?

Add a third battery and touch its button terminal with the free wire.

The bulb gets brighter and brighter because the batteries work together.

High voltage

Electricity from sockets in your house has a high voltage. It can be very dangerous. Only use batteries for your experiments.

Experiment batteries

For most experiments you can use three 1.5V batteries together, or one 4.5V battery. Here you can see some batteries with different terminals and how to join wires to them.

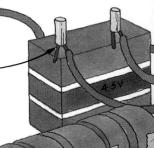

Wrap the wire ends around and tape them.

Hook wires around the terminals and screw the caps down.

Tape wires to both ends.

3

Flowing around

Electricity only flows if it can get all the way around from one terminal of the battery to the other. The path it follows is called a circuit. When electricity flows in a circuit it is called current.

Flowing through

Electric current flows through some things but not others. To see what it can flow through, set up a battery, bulb and three wires like this.

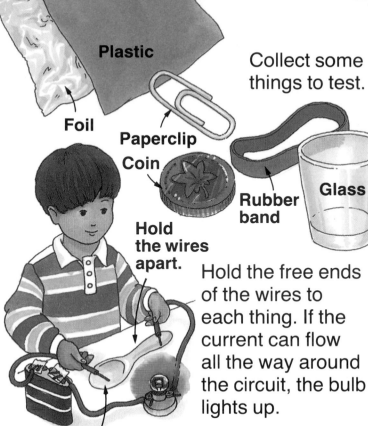

Plastic

Foil

Paperclip

Coin

Rubber band

Glass

Collect some things to test.

Hold the wires apart.

Hold the free ends of the wires to each thing. If the current can flow all the way around the circuit, the bulb lights up.

This wire joins the battery and bulb holder.

4·5V

Battery

There is a gap in this circuit. The current cannot jump across the gap, so the bulb is not lit.

Gap   **Both of these wires are free at one end.**

Current flows through this spoon.

You could make a chart to show your results. How many things that light the bulb are metal?

bulb lights	doesn't light
metal spoon	glass

Things that current flows through are called conductors. These are usually metal. Things current cannot flow through are called insulators.

Electrical wire

Most electrical wire is made of copper, which is a good conductor. It is often covered in an insulator such as plastic. This helps to make the electrical wire safe to use.

Pencil lead

There is a conductor called carbon in pencil lead. Some pencils have more carbon in them than others, so they are better conductors. See how bright the bulb is with different pencils.

Sharpen both ends.

Circuit maze

The current in this circuit flows through the foil. Which two corners would you touch with the wires to light the bulb?

You could make a circuit maze for your friends. Glue strips of foil onto cardboard. Make sure there is an unbroken path of foil between only two of the corners.

Foil

The answer is on page 74.

Inside a light bulb

Current can flow through a bulb because there are wires inside it. When it flows through a special coiled wire, the bulb lights.

Coiled wire

Wires

5

Turning on and off

You can make a switch for your circuits, to turn the lights on and off.

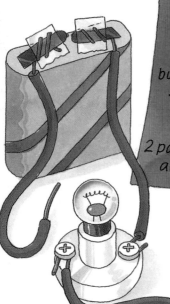

You need: battery, 3 wires, bulb in bulb holder, small piece of cardboard, paperclip, 2 paper fasteners, adhesive tape.

Join a battery, bulb and three wires like this.*

Push a paper fastener through the cardboard. Hook the paperclip onto the second fastener and push this fastener through the cardboard.

Make sure the paperclip can touch the first fastener.

*The same circuit is on page 4.

6

Turn the cardboard over. Wrap one wire around each paper fastener. Bend the legs of the fasteners back and tape them down.

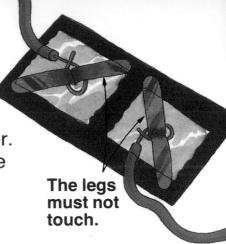

The legs must not touch.

When the paperclip touches both fasteners, the circuit is complete. Electricity can flow through the clip and fasteners, so the bulb lights up.

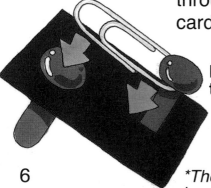

The paperclip and fasteners are good conductors.

Move the paperclip off one fastener to switch off the bulb. The current cannot flow now because the circuit is broken.

Turn the light on and off with your switch.

Scary face

Make a scary face to put over the bulb.

Turn a clear jar upside-down. Tape a see-through wrapper to one side.

Cut out a small face on a long piece of paper.

Tape the paper around the jar so the face is over the wrapper.

Cover the top with paper.

Fit the jar over the bulb. Turn the scary face light on and off with the switch.

Light hat

This light hat helps you to see in the dark.

Cut a cardboard strip long enough to go around your head so the ends overlap a little.

Set up a circuit with a switch on the cardboard like this. Tape everything down firmly.

You need: circuit with switch, plastic bottle (without cap), thin cardboard, foil, glue, adhesive tape.

Ask an adult to cut the top part off the bottle. Glue foil inside it. Tape the top over the bulb. Tape the ends of the cardboard together.

Bottle top

Foil   **Tape**

Switch   **Battery**

Bulb

Test your hat in the dark. Put it on your head and switch on the light.

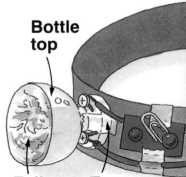

7

Flashing light switch

There are lots of different kinds of switches. Here you can find out how to make a flashing light switch.

Cut strips of foil about 2cm (1in) wide. Stick them onto the tube like this.

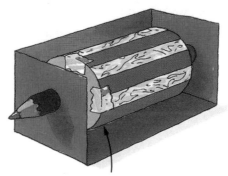

Make sure the tube doesn't touch the box.

Cut off part of the box so it looks like this. Make holes in the sides for the pencil to go through. Push the pencil through the holes.

The tube must fit inside the box.

Leave spaces between the strips.

Cut cardboard circles to cover the ends. Make a hole in the middle of each circle. Tape them onto the ends of the tube. Push the pencil through the holes and tape it in place.

Set up the bulb circuit as before. Ask an adult to strip 3cm (1½in) of plastic off the free ends of the wires.

Bare ends

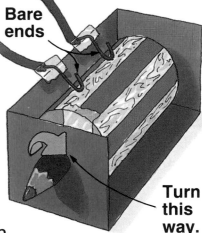

Bend these free ends upward. Tape them to the box so the metal part touches the tube.

Turn this way.

Turn the pencil to make the light flash. When the wires touch the foil, the circuit is complete and the bulb lights. When the wires touch the cardboard, the current cannot flow.

8

Flashing lighthouse

Here is a way to use a flashing light switch. Make a large tube with thin cardboard and tape it to make the lighthouse tower.

You could paint the tube.

Make the switch as before. Tape a carboard circle to the top of the tube. Tape the bulb and holder to the top.

You need to use longer wires than usual.

Tape a clear jar over the bulb. Make the lighthouse flash with the switch.

You could make a paper roof.

Use blue paper for the sea.

model dough rocks

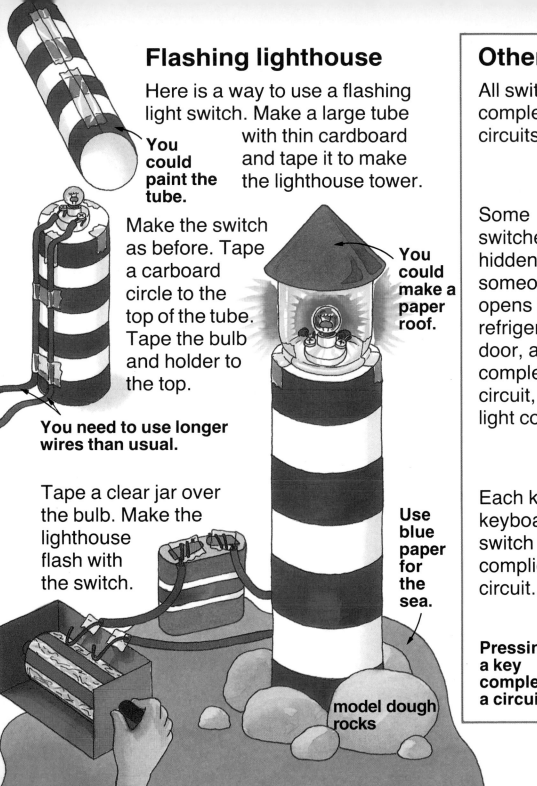

Other switches

All switches work by completing and breaking circuits.

Some switches are hidden. When someone opens this refrigerator door, a switch completes the circuit, so the light comes on.

Each key on a computer keyboard is a simple switch that controls a complicated circuit.

Pressing a key completes a circuit.

Other circuits

In these circuits the battery lights two bulbs at once.

Bulbs in a row

Join a wire to each battery terminal. Fasten a bulb and holder to each wire.

Join the bulb holders with a third wire so the bulbs light.

Are the lights as bright as usual?

The bulbs are dim because the current goes through one bulb and then the other. The battery has to work hard to light them both.

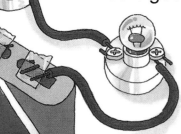

Take one bulb out of its holder.* You have broken the circuit, so the other bulb goes out.

This is called a series circuit.

*Never touch household bulbs when they are lit.

Brighter bulbs

Start by joining a wire to each terminal. Then twist two short wires onto the free end of each wire.

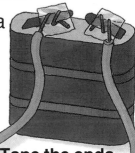

Tape the ends together.

Join a bulb and holder to each short wire on one side.

Christmas lights

Christmas tree lights are often in a series circuit. One broken bulb can stop the others from lighting.

Fasten the short wires on the other side to the bulb holders. How bright are the bulbs now?

The bulbs are bright because they are on different paths. The current only has to flow through one bulb on each path to get around the circuit.

Take one bulb out of its holder. What happens to the other bulb?

When you take out one bulb, the other stays lit. The current has another path to flow around the circuit.

This is a parallel circuit.*

*To stop your battery from running down, take the bulbs out.

Owl light

Draw an owl on cardboard and cut it out. Stick down circles of foil for the eyes. Push a pencil through them to make a hole in each eye.

You need: your parallel circuit, cardboard, foil, scissors, pencil, glue, adhesive tape.

The owl should be much larger than your battery.

Take the bulbs out of the holders. Tape the circuit to the back of the owl so the holders poke through the eyeholes.

Back of bulb holders

Tape

Screw the bulbs into the holders to turn on the light.

11

Making sound

Electricity does not just make light. It can make sound as well. Light and sound are both different kinds of energy.

Buzzer circuit

You can make sound with this circuit. You need a 6V buzzer, which you can buy at an electrical store.

Join a wire between one battery terminal and one of the buzzer wires. Join a second wire to the other side of the buzzer.

Free wire

Twist the wires together and tape them.

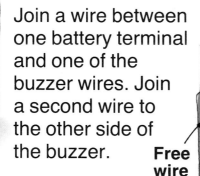

Other energy

Heat and movement are other kinds of energy that electricity can produce.

An electric motor makes this toy move.

Electricity makes heat in an electric iron.

Touch the free wire to the second terminal to set the buzzer off.

If your buzzer does not work, untwist the wires, turn the buzzer around and join it up again.

Buzzers make sound by making a thin metal strip shake very quickly. This movement is called vibration. You can feel it if you touch the buzzer.

Make a buzzer game

Set up a buzzer circuit. Then join a third wire to the battery, so there are two free ends in the circuit.

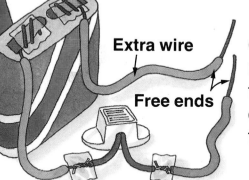

Extra wire

Free ends

Cover the bottom of the matchbox tray with foil and tape the free end of one wire to it. Tape the other wire to a piece of foil. Lay the foil over the matchbox.

Cut a slot in one end of the shoebox lid. Fit the tube into it.

Shoebox lid

Cut off the other end of the lid. Stick cotton reels* to the lid as obstacles.

Put two reels here.

Put books under both ends of the lid. The end with the tube should be higher.

This end is cut off.

Put the matchbox and circuit in front of the lower end of the lid.

Roll a marble through the tube, aiming it down the lid. If it lands in the matchbox, it knocks the pieces of foil together and completes the circuit. Can you set off the buzzer?

*Spools of thread (US)

13

Electricity and water

Electricity can flow through water. You can set up a circuit with water like this.

You need:
bulb circuit with 2 free wires (see page 4), bowl of water, foil, salt.

(see page 4)

Socket electricity

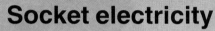

Electricity from sockets has such a high voltage that it can flow through tap water easily. Never touch plugs or sockets with wet hands.

Cut two large squares of foil. Hook each free wire in the circuit onto a square.

Put the foil squares into the water. Does the bulb light?

Don't let the squares touch.

A little current flows through the water, but not enough to light the bulb.

Stir in four big spoonfuls of salt. What happens?

Mixing salt and water makes a good conductor. Enough current flows through it to light the bulb.

Now use your circuit to see if electricity flows through dry salt. Does the bulb light?

Current flows through salty water, but dry salt is not a conductor.

Electrical timer

Try making an electrical timer, using salty water as a conductor.

You need:
wire, tall jar, salty water,
buzzer circuit (see page 12),
2 foil squares, adhesive tape,
empty dishwashing
liquid bottle.

Set up the buzzer circuit. Join an extra wire to the battery so there are two free wires. Hook each free end onto a foil square and hang them in the jar.

Tape

Extra wire

Leave about 7cm (3in) at the bottom.

Ask an adult to cut the bottle in half. Fill the top half with salty water.

Keep the cap on.

Open the cap and place the bottle over the jar. The salty water runs into the jar. When it reaches the foil, it completes the circuit and the buzzer goes off.

You can change how long the buzzer takes to go off by moving the pieces of foil up or down.

When the foil is higher, the timer takes longer.

You can use your timer for a game. Hide something. Can your friends find it before the buzzer goes off?

15

Making magnets

Electricity can turn iron or steel into magnets. You can use your battery to make a magnet like this.

You need:
battery and 2 wires,
2m (6½ ft) of thin
wire (see page 23),
bulb and holder,
switch (see page 6),
iron nail,
adhesive tape,
paperclip.

Wrap the thin wire tightly around the nail as many times as you can.

Tape the wire in place.

Hold the nail near a paperclip and turn on the switch. What happens?

The current makes the coil of wire magnetic. This turns the nail into a magnet, so it picks up the clip.

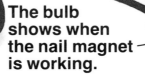

The bulb shows when the nail magnet is working.

Join the other wires to the battery terminals. Fasten one to the bulb holder and one to the switch.

Join one end of the wire around the nail to the switch, and the other to the bulb holder.

Turn off the switch. The clip falls off because the coil is only magnetic when current is flowing through it.*

Magnets made by electricity are called electromagnets. They are very useful because you can turn them on and off.

16

*The nail may still be a little magnetic. You can find out why on page 23.

Target game

You can make this target game with your electromagnet.

Make four small balls of model dough. Stick a paperclip into each one.

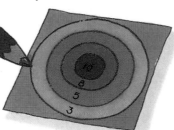

Draw a target. Number the rings like this.

Turn the box upside-down and put your circuit on it. Pick up each ball with the electromagnet. Hold it over the target and turn the switch off, so the ball falls onto the target.

If the ball does not fall at once, shake the nail.

The number in the ring where each ball lands gives your score.

Making electricity

Magnets are used to make electricity. When a magnet moves near a coil of wire, it makes electric current flow in the wire.

Bike lights

In a bicycle dynamo, the wheel turns a magnet near a coil. This makes current to light the lamp.

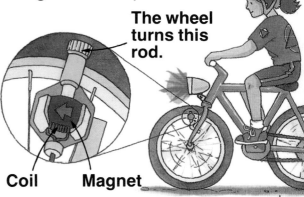

The wheel turns this rod.

Coil   **Magnet**

Generators

Electricity for houses is made in power stations by giant dynamos. They are called electric generators.

Power station

Batteries and meters

You can make a current meter using a compass. It shows when even a little electricity is flowing.

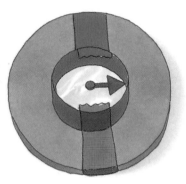

Tape the compass to a cardboard circle.

You need: small compass, 2m (6½ft) of thin wire (see page 23), cardboard, battery, scissors, adhesive tape.

Cut two slots in the cardboard. Wind the wire tightly around the compass at least 50 times.

Wind the wire inside the slots.

Join the wire ends to a battery. The current flows through the wire and makes it magnetic. This makes the compass needle move.

Make a battery

You can make a battery of your own. It is not strong enough to light a bulb, but you can test it with the current meter you have made.

You need: steel washer*, vinegar, coffee filter paper, shiny bronze coin, scissors, saucer.

Cut a circle of filter paper as big as the washer. Soak it in vinegar.

Filter paper

*You can get a washer from a hardware store.

Press the steel washer, paper, and bronze coin together.

Touch one wire from your meter to the washer and the other to the coin. The compass needle moves. This shows that the battery is making current.

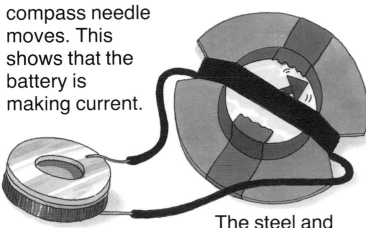

The steel and bronze are both conductors. The chemicals in the vinegar work together with them to make electric current. This only happens when the battery is in a circuit.

You can make the battery stronger by adding extra washers, paper and coins.

Put the layers in the same order.

Inside batteries

All batteries work like your home-made battery. Chemicals and two different conductors work together to make electricity.*

In this battery the two conductors are carbon and zinc. The carbon rod is joined to the terminal with + on it. This is called the positive terminal.

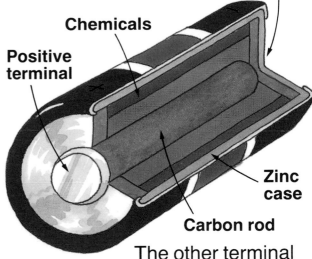

Negative terminal

Chemicals

Positive terminal

Zinc case

Carbon rod

The other terminal is part of the zinc case. It is marked with a −, and is called the negative terminal. The case also stops the chemicals in the battery from leaking out.

Never try to look inside a battery. The chemicals are dangerous.

Bright ideas

You can make lots of things using what you have learned about electricity.

Frog game

This game uses the idea that current only flows around a complete circuit (see page 4).

You need:
battery, wires,
6V buzzer (see page 12),
paper fasteners, thin cardboard,
crayons, scissors, adhesive tape.

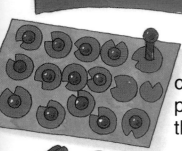

Draw lots of lily pads on the cardboard. Push paper fasteners through them.

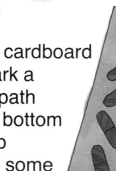

Turn the cardboard over. Mark a winding path from the bottom to the top between some fasteners.

20

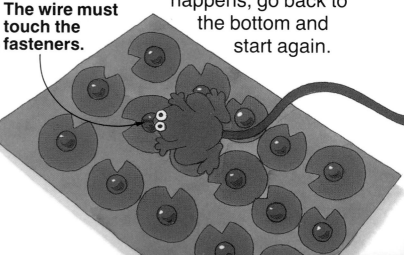

Join short wires between the other fasteners. Fasten the last wire to a battery terminal. Join the other terminal and the buzzer with a wire.

Join a long wire to the buzzer. Tape a paper frog shape to the free end.

The wire should stick out.

Turn the cardboard over. Try to get from the bottom to the top by moving the frog wire from one fastener to the next. The buzzer goes off if you land on a pad outside the path. When this happens, go back to the bottom and start again.

The wire must touch the fasteners.

Moon buggy

You can use the flashing light switch (page 8) in this buggy. Make the tube for the switch as before, but do not tape the pencil to the cardboard. This picture shows you how to make the buggy.

The light flashes when you push the buggy along.

Let the nails hang down onto the front roller.

Flag

Tape cardboard together to make the sides and top.

The back roller is a switch tube without foil strips.

Push the pencils through the sides. Stop them from turning with model dough.

Tape down the bulb circuit.

Wind each bare end around a nail*.

Foil strips on switch.

You could put a painted cardboard box over the buggy to turn it into a toy fire engine.

Hole for bulb

Cardboard box

Be an inventor

Can you think of other ways to change or improve the things you have made?

A switch here makes the owl on page 11 wink.

Copper nails work best.

Notes for parents and teachers

These notes will help to answer questions that arise from the activities on earlier pages.

Equipment

A battery that is too strong can burn out a bulb. This chart shows the right bulbs to use with different batteries.

Battery	Bulb
1.5 V	1.1 - 1.5 V
4.5 V (or three 1.5 V batteries together)	3 - 4.5 V
6 V	5 - 6.5 V

Use low voltage wire (not wire for household electricity). Here are some kinds of wire you can use.

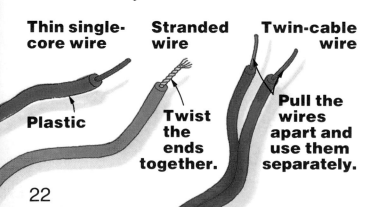

Thin single-core wire

Plastic

Stranded wire

Twist the ends together.

Twin-cable wire

Pull the wires apart and use them separately.

22

Looking at batteries (pages 2-3)

Electricity flowing through a wire is a stream of tiny invisible particles called electrons. A battery's voltage is a measure of how hard it pushes the electrons around a circuit.

Flowing around (pages 4-5)

Carbon is a conductor, although it is not a metal. Soft pencils – ones that produce darker lines – contain more carbon, so they are better conductors than hard pencils.

Hard pencils are marked H.

Soft pencils are marked B.

Bulbs

All conductors oppose, or resist, current to some extent. Thin wire resists current more than thick wire. The coiled wire inside bulbs, called the filament, is very thin, so it is difficult for current to flow through it. This makes the filament heat up and glow.

The filament glows white when it is hot.

Making sound (pages 12-13)

Sound, light, heat, movement and electricity are all forms of energy. Energy cannot be created or destroyed; it can only be turned into other forms of energy. Electricity is easy to turn into other kinds of energy.

Electricity and water (pages 14-15)

When things dissolve in water they split into tiny particles called ions. Ions can carry electrons through the water and complete a circuit. Tap water has small amounts of chemicals in it, so it contains ions. This means it can conduct electricity, but not as well as salty water.

Making magnets (pages 16-17)

You must use a bulb to make the electromagnet circuit safe. It stops the wires from getting too hot.

To make an electromagnet (and the current meter on page 18) use very thin covered wire. Thin plastic-covered wire called hook-up wire works well. Glazed copper wire, or magnet wire, is particularly good.

Glazed copper wire

Rub the ends with sandpaper until they are shiny.

Wires generate a magnetic field when current flows through them. Making the wire into a coil, or solenoid, strengthens the magnetic field. An iron or steel core, such as a nail, makes the field even stronger. The field turns the core into a magnet. Steel and some kinds of iron can stay magnetic even when the current is turned off.

Batteries and meters (pages 18-19)

Compass needles are magnets that normally point north/south. When one is near a solenoid, the needle reacts to its magnetic field.

Inside batteries

When the battery is in a circuit, a chemical reaction starts between the chemicals and the two conductors inside the battery. This produces ions which carry electrons to the negative terminal. The electrons travel around the circuit to the positive terminal.

The electrons move along the wire.

23

Then and now

This page shows some important electrical inventions and how they are used today.

Batteries

A scientist called Volta made the first battery in 1800. The word "volt" is named after him.

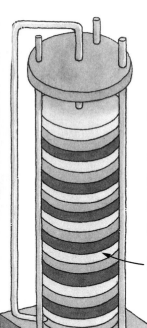

His battery was made of copper and zinc discs with pads soaked in chemicals between them. It worked just like the battery you made on pages 18 and 19.

— **Discs**

These days there are lots of different kinds of batteries. Some can even be recharged in a machine and used again.* They can be used up to 1,000 times.

Electric light

Edison made an electric lamp in 1879. The wire in it was made of carbon. It did not glow very brightly and burned away after 40 hours.

In modern bulbs the coiled wire is made of tungsten. It gets very hot and glows brightly without burning away.

Sun power

Some calculators use energy from the sun, or solar power, instead of batteries. A thin piece of material inside them makes electricity when light falls on it. This is called a solar cell.

Solar cells are used on space satellites. They make electricity when sunlight hits them.

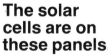

The solar cells are on these panels.

24   *Never try to recharge normal batteries, only rechargeable ones.*

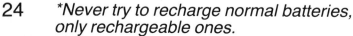

SCIENCE AND YOUR BODY

Consultant: Mary Dodge

Contents

About your body

This part of the book will help you find out more about your body and the different parts inside you that work to keep you alive. The first experiments are about skin.

Mending skin

When you hurt your skin, your body mends it. Your blood makes a scab to cover the place until new skin is ready.

Stretchy skin

Look at your hand. You can see how well your skin fits. It is creased where it needs to fold, and when you spread out your hand, it stretches.

Draw a caterpillar on the inside of your elbow with face paints.

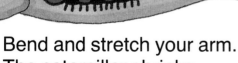

Bend and stretch your arm. The caterpillar shrinks and stretches with your skin.

Cooling down

You sweat when you are hot. Sweat is salty water that comes out of tiny holes in your skin. Try this to see what sweat is for.

Pour some water on the back of one hand. Keep the other one dry.

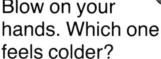

Blow on your hands. Which one feels colder?

The water cools you as it dries. Sweat cools you in the same way.

Fingerprinting

Your skin is different from other people's. Here is a way to prove this.

Press your finger on the sticky side of a piece of adhesive tape. Stick the tape onto another piece of paper.

Scribble very hard on a piece of paper with a pencil. Now rub the paper with a finger.

Keep your finger flat.

You have made a print that shows the pattern of the skin on your finger.

Make prints with your other fingers. They may make different patterns. Ask some friends to make fingerprints in the same way.

Prints for proof

The police keep a copy of criminals' fingerprints. They check if these prints appear at the scene of a crime, to prove who was involved.

Look closely at the fingerprints. No one else's will be quite like yours, unless you have a twin. Then your fingerprints may match.

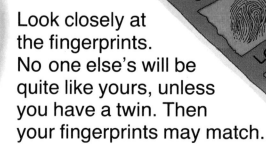

Me

Oliver

Leo

Touch

You feel things outside you with your skin. This is called your sense of touch. It tells you whether things are warm, cold, soft, hard, or scratchy.

Tickling test

Try tickling a friend gently in different places. Try his hands, feet, back, and elbows. Does it tickle as much in every place?

Your skin is more ticklish in some places than others. Ticklish places can feel light touches very easily.

Feeling things

You need different things of the same shape and size for this test. Here are some you could try.

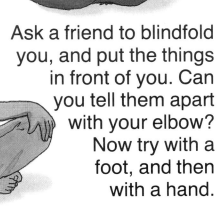

Bread roll

Tennis ball

Orange

Apple

Peach

Ask a friend to blindfold you, and put the things in front of you. Can you tell them apart with your elbow? Now try with a foot, and then with a hand.

It is hard to feel differences between things with your elbows.

Most people's feet are very ticklish, but not very good at telling things apart.

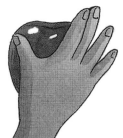

Your hands can feel small differences between things. They are a very sensitive part of your body.

Cold touch

Hold one hand in a bowl of ice cubes. Count to 30. Now dry your hand and try to pick up some grains of rice.

It is hard to pick up the rice because your sense of touch does not work as well when your skin is cold.

Fool your senses

Fill three big bowls with water – one hot, one cold and one warm. Put the warm one in the middle.

Put one hand in the cold bowl and one in the hot. Count to 30. Now move both hands to the middle bowl. Does the water feel hot or cold?

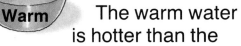

The warm water is hotter than the cold water. It feels hot to the hand that came from the cold bowl.

The same water feels cold to your other hand, because it is colder than the water in the hot bowl. Your sense of touch only tells you how the water in the middle bowl feels different to each hand.

Reading hands

Braille is a sort of printing, made of patterns of raised dots on thick paper. Blind people read it with their hands. They read by recognizing the different patterns.

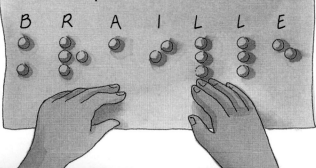

29

Looking out

Your eyes need light for you to see. Try these experiments to find out more about how you see.

Light and dark

Take some crayons into an unlit room at night. You can see a little after a while, because there is always some light.

Look at the crayons. How easy is it to tell them apart?

Now turn on the light. Can you tell the crayons apart now?

When there is only a little light you can see the shapes of things but not whether they are red, blue, green or orange. You need more light to see this too.

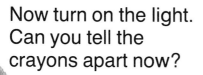

Seeing sideways

Look straight ahead. Ask a friend to move a pencil all the way around your head, level with your eyes. Tell him when you see it appear and disappear.

Keep your head still.

You can see things at the side of your head as well as in front of you, even if you are only looking ahead.

Seeing all around

Some animals, like mice, have eyes on the sides of their heads. They can see almost all around to keep a look-out for danger.

Two views

Each of your eyes sees a different view.

Hold up a pencil, and close one eye. Line the pencil up with something in the distance. Now swap eyes without moving the pencil.

Left eye closed

Right eye closed

The pencil seems to jump, because each of your eyes sees it from a different place.

When both of your eyes are open, your brain puts together the two views that they see. This makes one very clear picture.

Tricky pictures

You cannot always trust what you see. Here are some pictures that may confuse you. They are called optical illusions.

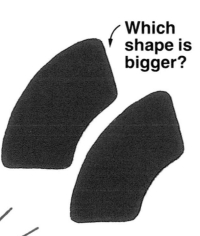

Which shape is bigger?

Are these red lines straight?

Use a ruler to find out if you are right.

Looking both ways

Chameleons' eyes can look in opposite directions at the same time. Nobody knows how their brains make sense of the pictures.

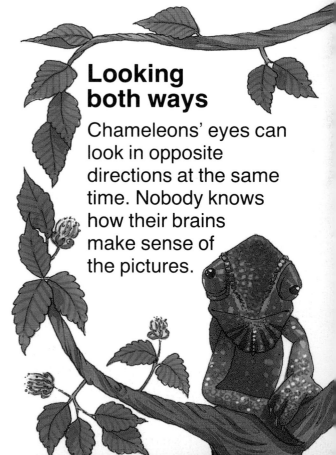

Speaking out

Your voice is made in your throat. It comes out through your mouth.

Feel your voice

There is a ridged lump in the front of your neck. Touch it. If you sing you can feel it moving.

There are two stretchy flaps of skin in this ridged lump. They are called your vocal cords. They wobble as air moves past them. This is called vibrating. It makes the sound of your voice.

This shows the ridged lump in your throat. It is part of the tube your breath comes through.

Vocal cords

If you could see down your throat, your vocal cords would look a bit like this.

Balloon voice

Blow up a balloon. Stretch its neck tightly and let the air out. What do you hear?

The balloon squeals because the escaping air makes its stretched neck vibrate. It stops squealing as the air runs out.

Make a small cardboard tube and put it in the balloon's neck. Blow it up again. Now it does not squeal as the air escapes. The tube holds the sides of the neck still, so they cannot vibrate.

Muscles stretch your vocal cords when you speak. When your vocal cords are not stretched, they are still, so they do not make a noise.

Seeing vibrations

Stretch a rubber band between your hands. Pluck it with your thumb, to make a sound. You can see the band vibrating.

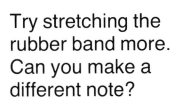

Try stretching the rubber band more. Can you make a different note?

Your vocal cords vibrate like rubber bands. When they are tightly stretched, they make a high note. When they are less stretched, they make a lower note.

Cricket songs

Other creatures make sounds in very different ways. Bush crickets make a singing noise by rubbing their wings together to make them vibrate.

Shaping sounds

If you want to make different sounds, you need to use your mouth as well as your vocal cords.

Sing a note. Push your lips out while you are singing, then smile broadly. You can hear the sound you are making change to "oo", and then to "ee".

The sound changes as you change the shape of your mouth and your lips.

33

In your ears

Your ears help you hear, and they help you balance. All the working parts are hidden inside your head.

This part helps you balance.

Ear-drum

Sounds go in through this hole.

This is the only part outside your head.

Feeling sound

Hold a balloon in front of your mouth, and sing. What can you feel?

The sound of you singing travels through the air. It hits the balloon's skin and makes it wobble, or vibrate.

Your ear-drum is a stretchy part inside your ear. It vibrates when sounds hit it, like the balloon. Your brain can tell what sounds make the vibrations.

Catching sound

Hold your hands in front of your ears, like this, and talk. Still talking, move your hands behind your ears. Can you hear better now?

Hands in front of your ears stop sounds from your mouth from getting into your ears.

Hands behind your ears catch the sounds so they go into your ears. This helps you to hear your voice better.

Keeping your balance

There are tiny curved tubes in your ears with liquid inside them. Your brain can tell from the way the liquid moves how you are changing position. You can notice any sudden change and stop yourself from falling over.

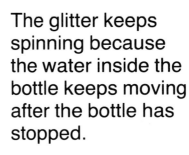

The tubes look like this.

Pour some water into a bottle and move it around. The water moves as you change the bottle's position, like the liquid in your balance tubes.

Getting dizzy

Spin around ten times in a place where you won't hurt yourself if you fall over. When you stop, you feel dizzy.

To see why it happens, fill a see-through plastic bottle with water. Shake in some glitter, and put on the lid.

Spin the bottle, then stop it quickly. Does the glitter stop spinning too?

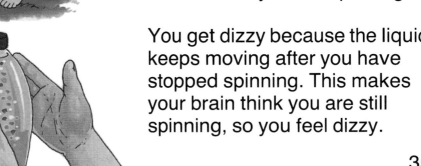

The glitter keeps spinning because the water inside the bottle keeps moving after the bottle has stopped.

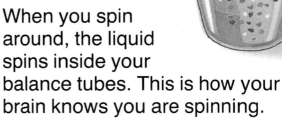

When you spin around, the liquid spins inside your balance tubes. This is how your brain knows you are spinning.

You get dizzy because the liquid keeps moving after you have stopped spinning. This makes your brain think you are still spinning, so you feel dizzy.

35

Breathing

There are two big spongy bags in your chest called lungs. Each time you breathe, your lungs fill with air and empty again.

This shows where your lungs are inside you.

In and out

Lie on your back. Put one hand on your chest and one on your stomach. Breathe deeply. Can you feel your chest and stomach move?

Bones called ribs move to make your chest bigger and smaller. A muscle under your chest helps by moving up and down. It is called your diaphragm (say die-a-fram).

Breathing model

You can make air move in and out of this model.

1. Ask an adult to cut a see-through plastic bottle in half. Stretch a balloon over the neck, and push it inside.

2. Stretch a piece of a plastic bag over the open end of the bottle. Tape it all around so there are no gaps.

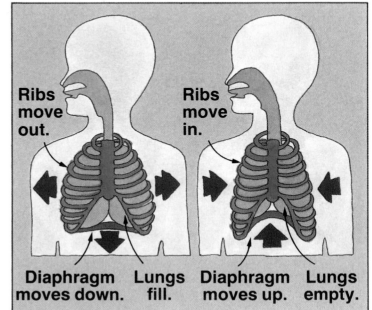

Ribs move out.

Ribs move in.

Diaphragm moves down. **Lungs fill.** **Diaphragm moves up.** **Lungs empty.**

3. Tape a strip of paper to the middle of the plastic.

4. Pull down the plastic by pulling the strip, then push it up again. What happens to the balloon?

When you pull the strip down, you make the space around the balloon bigger. Air moves into the balloon to fill the extra space.

When you push it up again, you make the space smaller again, and push out the air.

Your lungs fill with air in the same way. When your chest gets bigger, air moves into your lungs. When it gets smaller, the air is pushed out again.

How much air?

Fill a see-through plastic bottle with water. Put on the lid. Hold it upside down in a bowl of water and take off the lid.

Don't let in any air.

Push a bendy straw into the neck of the bottle. Hold the bottle upright. Breathe in, then blow gently into the straw.

Don't let the straw come out.

All the air you blow out collects at the top of the bottle. You can see how much air there is in one breath.

Bones and muscles

Lots of different kinds of bones fit together inside your body. They make a framework that holds you up. It is called your skeleton.

Bending

You can bend in the places where your bones fit together. These places are called joints.

Try moving around without bending your arms and legs. Can you sit down? Can you get up again? How about scratching your head?

Now bend your arms and legs. Some joints only bend up and down. Others can move in a circle.

38

Make a model arm

You can make a model joint that bends up and down like your elbow.

Cut two strips of cardboard, one twice as wide as the other. Give the narrow strip one rounded end.

Fold the wide strip in half lengthwise. Put the rounded end of the other strip in the fold. Join them with a paper fastener.

Rounded end

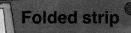
Folded strip

Tape a paper hand onto the end of the folded strip of cardboard.

This model can only bend one way, like your elbow. Can you think of another joint that bends this way?*

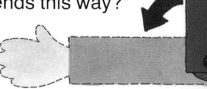

* Answer on page 74

Moving your bones

Muscles are joined to bones. They make bones move by pulling them up and down. You can make string muscles for your model arm.

Tape here.

Cut two pieces of thick string the same length. Tape a piece to each side of your model arm, like this.

Tape this piece higher up.

Pull one string, then the other. Can you make the model move?

Muscles pull on bones. They cannot push, so they have to work in pairs. One muscle pulls in each direction, like the strings on your model.

Top muscle pulls to bend arm.

Bottom muscle pulls to straighten arm.

Muscles change shape to pull on bones. They bunch up and become shorter.

Broken bones

If you break a bone, your body can mend it. You have to wear a plaster cast so the broken ends line up properly.

Bend your arm. You can feel the muscle on top bunch up and go stiff. Then stretch your arm out hard. Feel how stiff the muscle underneath becomes.

Clench your fist.

39

Feeding your body

Everything you eat goes into your stomach and through some very long tubes inside you. Along the way, your body changes the food so it is easy to use.

Stomach

These tubes are called intestines.

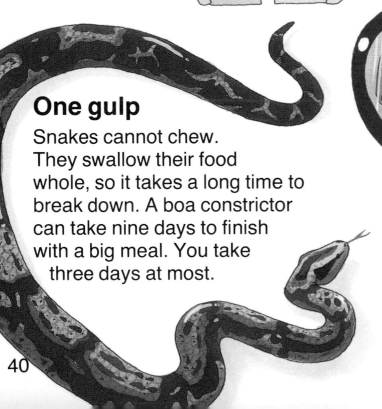

Biting and chewing

Take a bite out of an apple. Which teeth do you bite it with? Now chew the piece you have bitten off. Do you chew it with the same teeth?

Look at your mouth in a mirror. Are your front teeth the same shape as the back ones?

Your front teeth are sharp-edged, for cutting through food.

Back teeth are big and lumpy, for grinding food into tiny pieces.

One gulp

Snakes cannot chew. They swallow their food whole, so it takes a long time to break down. A boa constrictor can take nine days to finish with a big meal. You take three days at most.

Chewing grinds food into small pieces and mixes it with your spit, or saliva. This makes the food easy to swallow.

Breaking down

There are chemicals in your saliva and in your stomach to break down food. They are called enzymes. Try this to see what enzymes can do.

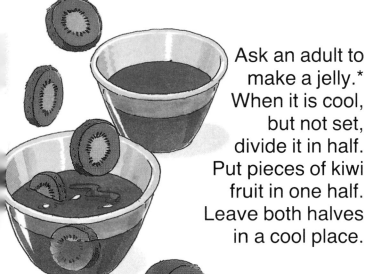

Ask an adult to make a jelly.* When it is cool, but not set, divide it in half. Put pieces of kiwi fruit in one half. Leave both halves in a cool place.

Look at the jellies after a few hours. Have they both set?

There is an enzyme in kiwi fruit that breaks down jelly. This stops it from setting.

*Also called gelatin (US).

Groans and gurgles

Sometimes your stomach rumbles after a meal. What you hear is the noise of food and air going along the tubes inside you.

Enzymes break down the food in your stomach into very tiny pieces, so they make a sort of soup.

Your blood takes these tiny pieces of food from your intestines to other parts of your body. You get rid of what you don't need when you go to the toilet.

41

Pumping blood

If you put your ear to a friend's chest, you can hear thumping. It is his heart beating. Each time it beats it fills with blood and squeezes it out again. The blood moves inside tubes called blood vessels.

What blood carries

Your blood carries oxygen from the air you breathe. It takes the oxygen to your muscles, along with tiny pieces of food. The muscles use the oxygen and food to make energy.

This picture shows where your heart and blood vessels are inside you.

Networks of blood vessels take blood to your lungs.

Your heart is slightly on the left side of your body.

Your blood vessels reach all over your body.

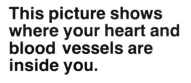

Pumping hard

Your heart pumps your blood very strongly. You can even feel the beating in your arm.

Hold two fingers on your wrist, like this. Can you feel a regular throbbing?

Your fingers are over a blood vessel near the surface. You can feel the blood moving through the blood vessel. This beating is called your pulse.

Fast and slow

Flatten a small ball of model dough and stick a toothpick in the middle.

Relax your arm and rest your hand on a table. Balance the model dough on your wrist, where you can feel your pulse. Can you see the toothpick move?

The toothpick moves each time your heart beats and pushes blood through the blood vessel. Count how many times it moves in 30 seconds. Then take off the toothpick.

You need a watch that shows seconds.

Squeezing hard

Your heart is about the size of your fist. Try this to see how strong it is.

Squeeze a tennis ball in one hand. Can you squash it?

Each time your heart beats, it squeezes as hard as you need to squeeze to squash the ball.

Walk quickly for a while. Balance the model dough on your wrist again. Now how many times does the toothpick move in 30 seconds?

When you exercise, your heart beats faster to send the blood around more quickly. Your muscles need more food and oxygen to make energy because they are using it up faster.

43

In control

Your brain is inside your head. It tells every part of your body what to do, even when you are asleep.

A bony case called your skull protects your brain.

Reaction timer

When you catch something, your brain sends a message to your hand, telling it to catch. The faster the message travels, the faster you move, or react. You can test your reactions.

Cut a long thin piece of stiff cardboard. Draw lines across it and mark the top. This is your reaction timer.

Hold up the timer. Ask a friend to hold his hand near the bottom without quite touching it. Ask him to catch it when you drop it.

Write his name on the mark where he catches it. Then ask him to drop the timer for you.

Dreaming

Dreams can be strange, but scientists think they are your brain's way of making sense of things – either things that happened during the day, or even things you hear or feel in your sleep.

The nearer the bottom you catch the timer, the faster your reactions are.

Automatic reactions

Your brain can make your body do lots of things without you even thinking about them. These automatic reactions are called reflexes. Ask a friend to help you make a reflex work.

Blinking

You blink automatically. Every time you blink, water washes your eyes. It wipes away dust and other things that might hurt your eyes.

Make a room dim by closing the curtains, then look at yourself in a mirror. Look at the middle of your eyes. The black parts in the middle are called your pupils.

Pupil

Can you see how big your pupils are? They get bigger in the dark to let in more light. This helps you to see better.

Now ask a friend to turn on the light. Watch your eyes very carefully in the mirror. What happens to your pupils?

Your pupils shrink automatically when the light gets stronger. Your brain makes them close up to keep too much light from getting into your eyes, because it could harm them.

Notes for parents and teachers

These notes will help answer questions that arise from the activities on earlier pages.

About your body (pages 26-27)

Your fingerprints are different from other people's because of a special code in every cell in your body, made of a chemical called DNA. This code tells your body how to grow – for example, whether you have blue eyes, and how tall you will be. It is a very complicated code and everyone's is different, except for identical twins, who may have the same fingerprints.

Touch (pages 28-29)

The ends of nerves in your skin, called receptors, send messages to your brain about what they feel. Some nerve endings detect pressure, some heat, cold, or pain. How sensitive any area of your skin is depends on how close together the nerve endings are. They are closest together in your fingertips and parts of your face, like your lips. This is why they are the most sensitive parts of your body.

Looking out (pages 30-31)

Light reflected off things goes into your eye through a hole called the pupil. Nerves inside your eye detect the light as it hits the back of your eye, and send a message to your brain about it. The brain interprets the pattern of the light as an image.

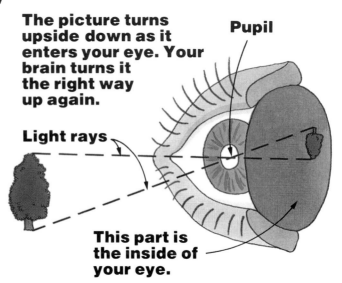

The picture turns upside down as it enters your eye. Your brain turns it the right way up again.

Pupil

Light rays

This part is the inside of your eye.

Speaking out (pages 32-33)

As the vocal cords are stretched and relaxed by the muscles around them, their edges become thinner and thicker. Thinner edges make a higher noise. Thicker ones make lower notes. Men have thicker, longer vocal cords than women. This is why they tend to have deeper voices.

Breathing (pages 36-37)

Air is a mixture of gases, one of which is called oxygen. It is the only part of air that your body uses. Oxygen from the air passes into your blood through the walls of your lungs. Your blood takes it to your muscles. They use it to make energy, producing a waste gas called carbon dioxide. Your blood takes the carbon dioxide back to your lungs and you breathe it out.

Pumping blood (pages 42-43)

You have big blood vessels close to your heart, which branch off into smaller and smaller vessels, to reach every part of your body. Blood travels away from your heart in blood vessels called arteries, and back to your heart in veins.

Your heart is a very strong muscle. Like all your other muscles, it needs blood to bring it oxygen and food, and exercise to keep fit.

Bones and muscles (pages 38-39)

Wrist joint

Spine

Ball and socket joint

There are lots of different types of joints between your bones. Your knees and elbows are like hinges. Your hips and shoulders are made like a ball in a socket, so they can turn in a circle. Your wrists have lots of small sliding bones in them to help them move to different positions easily. The joints in your spine enable it to curve but not bend at a sharp angle.

In control (pages 44-45)

Different parts of your brain do different jobs. One part works all the time to make sure you keep breathing. It also regulates your heartbeat. Other parts control speech and movement, thinking and memory. This shows you the jobs some parts of the brain do.

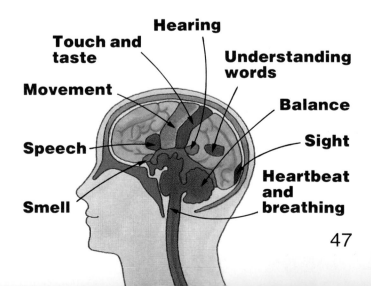

Hearing

Touch and taste

Understanding words

Movement

Balance

Speech

Sight

Heartbeat and breathing

Smell

47

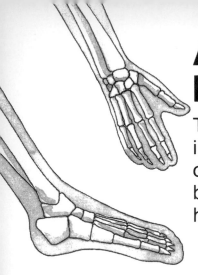

Amazing body facts

There are 206 bones in your skeleton. Just over half of these bones are in your hands and feet.

There are so many blood vessels in your body that if you stretched them out end to end, they would reach right around the Earth.

The hardest substance in your body is the covering on your teeth. This is called enamel.

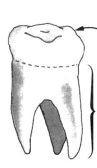

Enamel

This part holds your tooth in your jaw.

Roughly two-thirds of your body is made up of water.

Your heart beats roughly 5500 times an hour. Adults' hearts beat more slowly – about 3400 times an hour.

The hairs on your head can grow up to 12mm (½in) a month. Most people's hair cannot grow longer than 1m (39in), but some people can grow their hair down to their feet.

Sneezes can travel at 95km per hour (60 miles per hour).

SCIENCE WITH WEATHER

Rebecca Heddle and Paul Shipton

Consultant: Dave Kennedy BSc, Dip Ed

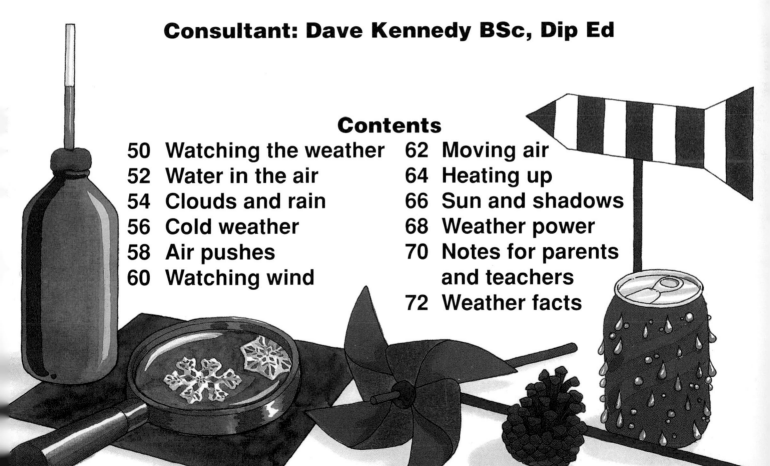

Contents

Watching the weather

Next time you are outside, look at the weather. It may be sunny or raining, windy or still. Whatever is happening, it can change – sometimes very suddenly. This part of the book is all about weather and how it can change.

Weather diary

Watch the weather every day. You can draw pictures in a weather diary to show what the weather is like.

Does the weather change much from day to day?

Rainy days

When it is raining, but not thundering*, go out with an umbrella. What happens to the rain when it hits the ground?

Some rain soaks in and makes mud.

Some water lies on the ground as puddles.

Can you see any animals or birds? They tend to hide from the rain.

It can rain so hard that it knocks leaves off trees. Sometimes the raindrops are so small you cannot hear them on your umbrella.

*Do not take shelter under trees when there is thunder and lightning.

Measuring rain

You can make a rain gauge from an empty plastic bottle, and use it to measure how much rain falls each day.

Ask an adult to cut the bottle in half. Stand the top half upside down in the bottom.

This part stops things from falling into the rain you collect.

Stand your rain gauge outside, in the open. Put stones around it to keep it upright.

Use a ruler.

Measure how much water there is in your rain gauge every day, then empty it. Record it in your weather diary.

Try to guess how much water there will be in the rain gauge before you look. There will often be much less than you think.

Forecasting

Scientists study the weather. They learn how it is likely to change, and make forecasts which tell people what it may do.

If you see a weather forecast on television, wait and see how close it is to what happens where you live.

Floods

When it rains very hard for a long time, the water cannot run away. Rivers get much deeper and may overflow.

51

Water in the air

When it rains, some water soaks into the ground, but some is left as puddles. Try this to see what happens to puddles when it stops raining.*

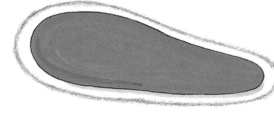

Is the puddle the same size an hour later?

Draw around a puddle with chalk.

It is smaller because some of the water has escaped into the air.

Where the puddle goes

Water in the puddle turns into tiny droplets which are too small to see. The droplets are very light, so they float into the air. This is called evaporation.

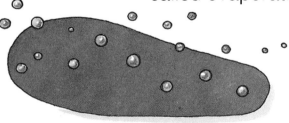

Drying out

Wind and warmth make water evaporate more quickly. This is why clothes dry best on windy days when it is warm and sunny.

The air is always full of water that has evaporated from rivers, seas and the ground.

52   *It will only work if it does not start raining again.

How much water?

You can see how much water there is in the air by looking at pine cones. They open out in dry air, and close up when it is damp.

People say closed pine cones mean rain.

When there is lots of water in the air, it often means that it will rain soon.

Water from the air

Leave a can of drink in the refrigerator overnight. See what happens when you take it out the next day.

The can cools the air around it. Cold air cannot hold as much water. The invisible water droplets in the air join into bigger drops that you can see. This is called condensation.

You can see the drops on the can.

Hot and sticky

Warm air can hold lots of water. The air in tropical places holds so much water that it can make you feel sticky.

Dew

Dew often forms on grass after a warm, dry day. It is water from the air near the ground which condenses as the air cools.

Dew can form on anything near the ground.

Clouds and rain

There is water in your breath. You can see this water as a little cloud when you are out on a cold day.

Tiny water droplets in your breath condense in the cold air (see page 53). They become drops big enough to see, but small enough for the air to hold up.

(see page 53)

How clouds form

Air gets cooler as it rises, and the water droplets in it condense and get bigger. The drops of water gather together to make clouds.

The air is colder high up.

Fog is really a cloud at ground level. Fog that is not very thick is called mist.

Making rain

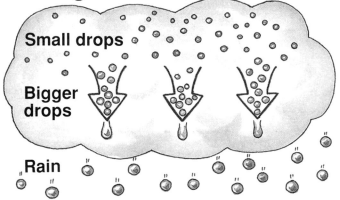

Small drops

Bigger drops

Rain

The drops of water inside a cloud bump into each other and join together. When the drops become too heavy for the air to hold up, they fall as rain.

Up and down

You can make a mini-rainfall in a bowl of hot water. Cover it with plastic food wrap and put ice cubes on top.

Some of the hot water evaporates. It turns into tiny invisible droplets.

The water droplets hit the cold plastic and condense into drops. They join together to make bigger drops. Then they fall back into the water.

Water evaporates from seas, rivers and the soil.

The invisible droplets condense and make clouds.

The water falls back as rain.

The water in the world goes around like this all the time.

Reading clouds

Different types of cloud can bring different sorts of weather. You can forecast what the weather may be like from which clouds you can see coming.

A low blanket of grey clouds can bring light rain.

Dark clouds like this thunder-cloud hold lots of water. They mean it may be stormy.

Small white fluffy clouds usually mean fine weather.

Cold weather

When water gets very cold it freezes and turns into ice. In cold weather the water in ponds, lakes and even rivers can freeze.*

Dripping water can turn into icicles.

Ice power

Fill a plastic bottle with water. Put a coin across the top. Leave it upright in the freezer overnight.

The ice lifts the coin because water gets bigger as it freezes.

Burst pipes

Water pipes can burst if the water inside them freezes and pushes against the sides. Most water pipes are wrapped in thick material to keep out the cold.

Frost

On cold mornings you may see frost on the ground and trees, and on car windows.

You can scrape frost with a stick. It can be so thin that you can melt it by breathing hard on it.

Frost is made up of tiny ice crystals that sparkle.

Sometimes the crystals make patterns.

56

Never try to walk on frozen ponds or streams.

Snow

When it is cold enough, the water in the air freezes to start snowflakes. These grow in the clouds until they are big enough to fall.

You can cool black paper in a freezer and catch snowflakes on it. Look at them with a magnifying glass.

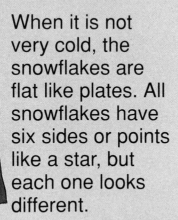

When it is not very cold, the snowflakes are flat like plates. All snowflakes have six sides or points like a star, but each one looks different.

When it is very cold, the snow is powdery. The snowflakes are small and sometimes shaped like needles.

How much snow?

Fill a container with snow. Do not pack it down.

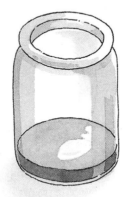

Let the snow melt. How much water was it made of?

Snow takes up much more space than water because there is lots of air inside it.

When you make a snowball or tread on snow, you pack it down and squeeze the air out of it.

57

Air pushes

We cannot see air, but it is all around us and pushes against everything all the time.

Pushing air trick

Fill a plastic cup to the brim with water.

Put a postcard on top of the cup and push it down.

Quickly turn the cup upside down, still holding the postcard in place. Now let go of the postcard.

Do this over the sink.

The postcard stays under the cup because air pushes up against it. Air pushes from underneath things as well as from on top. It pushes so strongly it can keep the water in the cup.

58

Make a barometer

Sometimes the air pushes harder than at other times. The amount it pushes is called air pressure. Barometers show when the air pressure changes.

You need: empty jar, balloon, rubber band, drinking straw, adhesive tape, cardboard.

Cut the neck off the balloon. Stretch the balloon over the top of the jar. Fasten it tightly with a rubber band so that air cannot get in or out.

Tape one end of the straw to the middle of the balloon. Cut the other end to make a point.

Tape a piece of cardboard to the jar, and mark where the end of the straw points.

If the weather changes, look at your barometer again. Is the straw still pointing at the same place?

The air pressure and the weather in a place often change at the same time.

How the barometer works

The barometer shows when the air pressure outside the jar becomes higher or lower. When it becomes higher, the air pushes down hard on the balloon.

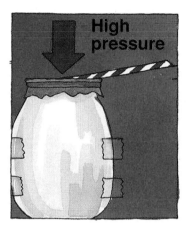

High pressure

The end of the straw points up when the air pushes the balloon down.

When the air pressure is lower, the air inside the jar pushes up on the balloon more than the air outside pushes down.

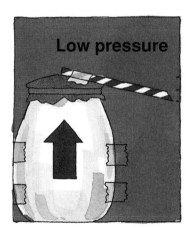

Low pressure

The air pressure is often high when the sky is clear, and low when the weather is cloudy.

Watching wind

You cannot see the wind, but you can see it moving trees, clouds and smoke. Here is something you can make to show how hard the wind is blowing.

Paint one cup and let it dry. Then tape the cups to the edges of the plate.

The cups should all face the same way. →

Tape the cotton reel to the middle of the plate, on the other side from the cups.

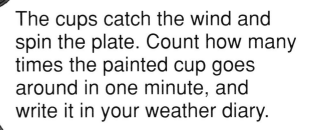

Push the stick into the ground and slot the cotton reel on top of it.

The cups catch the wind and spin the plate. Count how many times the painted cup goes around in one minute, and write it in your weather diary.

Bring it in if it starts raining.

See how many times the plate spins on different days. The faster the cups go around, the stronger the wind is.

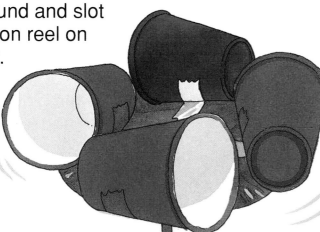

60

*empty spool of thread (US)

Wind directions

Winds are named after the direction they come from – north winds blow from the north. You can make a weather vane to show the direction of the wind.

You need:
stiff cardboard,
knitting needle,
pen top,
adhesive tape,
paper,
compass.

Cut out a cardboard arrow with one wide end and one narrow end, like this.

Tape the pen top to the arrow. Put the pen top on the point of the needle. The arrow should move freely to point at you when you blow at it.

Powerful wind

The strongest winds are called hurricanes. They can break up buildings and knock down trees.

Push the needle through a piece of paper into the ground. Use a compass* to check the directions, and mark the compass points on the paper.

Weigh down the corners with stones.

When the wind blows, the arrow points into the wind. See if the wind often blows from the same direction.

You could ask an adult to help you use the compass.

61

Moving air

Wind is moving air. When air heats up, it rises. Try these experiments to see how air moves.

Warm air propellor

1. Draw a circle on paper, around a reel of tape. Cut it out and fold it in half twice.

2. Unfold the paper and thread a piece of thin string through it where the folds cross. Knot one end.

Gliding

Sometimes you can see birds rising without flapping their wings. They are flying in warm air. It pushes them up as it rises.

3. Cut slits around the edge, to make blades. With the knot on top, bend up one side of each blade so it looks like this.

4. Dangle the propellor over a warm heater*, holding the string. You can see how it swings and twirls.

Warming air

The Sun's heat warms the air in some places more than others. This makes patches of warm air that rise.

The heater warms the air above it, so the air rises. It pushes past the propellor's blades and makes it turn.

*Don't let the paper touch the heater.

62

Making wind

Try this experiment to make a wind. Blow up a balloon and hold the neck shut. Feel the side of the balloon.

You can feel the air pushing out strongly, because it is squashed into the balloon. It is at higher pressure than the air around it.*

Tornadoes

A tornado is a powerful, spinning wind that has very low pressure inside it. It sucks up things in its path, like a huge vacuum cleaner.

Now let the air out of the balloon, holding a hand in front of the neck.

You can feel the air rushing out of the balloon, to even out the pressure. You have made a sort of wind.

Wind always evens out pressure. When warm air rises, it pushes less hard on the things underneath it – the pressure there is lower.

Warm air rises.

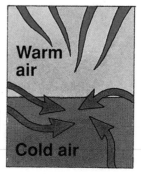

Warm air

Cold air

Cold air moves in from the places around where the pressure is higher. We feel the movement of the air as wind.

*See pages 58–59 for more about air pressure.

Heating up

The Earth gets light and heat from the Sun. The Sun is a giant ball of burning gases many times bigger than the Earth.

The Earth is surrounded by a layer of gases called the atmosphere.

The Sun's rays pass through the atmosphere and heat the Earth. Some heat from the Earth goes back into space, but the atmosphere traps some.

Atmosphere

The earth is shaped like a ball.

Sun's rays

Some heat cannot escape.

The way this heat is trapped is called the greenhouse effect. Without it the Earth would be too cold for us to live.

Greenhouse experiment

Put two ice cubes on saucers. Stand a glass over one and put them both in a sunny place.

Look at the ice cubes every five minutes. Which do you think will melt first?

Some heat cannot escape from the glass.

The glass traps some heat, so the ice under it melts first.

Hotter and hotter

Pollution has changed the Earth's atmosphere so it traps more heat. This will probably make the Earth hotter.

64

Hot and cold

The temperature is how hot or cold the weather is. People measure the temperature with a thermometer. You can make a simple one to see how it works.

Fill a plastic bottle with water. Add some food dye.

Wrap model dough around a clear straw.

Make sure you don't squash the straw.

Put the straw in the bottle, and squash down the model dough so it seals the bottle. This is your thermometer.

Using thermometers

Most thermometers have liquid inside them that gets bigger when the air is warmer. They can show even small changes in temperature.

Look at a thermometer to see how hot it is.

The higher the liquid is, the hotter the day.

Stand your thermometer in a bowl of hot water. Watch what happens to the water in the straw.

Now stand the thermometer in icy water.

When the water gets hot it takes up more space and moves up the straw. It shrinks again when it cools.

Sun and shadows

Stand in a sunny place in the morning, with your back to the Sun*. Ask a friend to draw around your shadow in chalk.

Do this again in the same place at lunchtime, and in the afternoon. Is your shadow always the same length? Where does it point?

Morning

Midday

Your shadow shows where you block the sunlight.

Afternoon

Your shadow moves, shrinks and grows because the Sun's light comes from different directions through the day.

66

Why shadows change

Stick a straw to a big ball with model dough. Slowly turn the ball in the light of a small lamp. Watch the straw's shadow move.

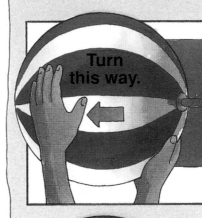

Turn this way.

The shadow is short when the straw points straight at the light.

The shadow grows longer as the ball turns and the straw points away.

The Earth turns in the Sun's light once a day. Your shadow changes like the straw's as the light comes from above you or from one side.

Never look straight at the Sun. It can damage your eyes.

Summer and winter

There are seasons because the Earth tilts like this.

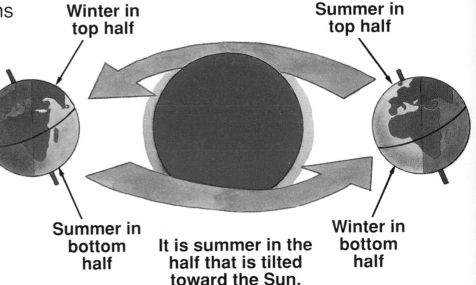

Winter in top half

Summer in top half

Summer in bottom half

Winter in bottom half

It is summer in the half that is tilted toward the Sun.

As well as turning once a day, the Earth moves around the Sun once a year. Because of the way it tilts, different parts of the Earth are closer to the Sun at different times of year.

Hot and cool

Rays of sunlight slant across the half of the Earth that leans away from the Sun. The rays spread out over a large area, so they do not heat it up much.

The Sun's rays shine more directly on the half of the Earth that is tilted toward it. Direct rays make the land hotter.

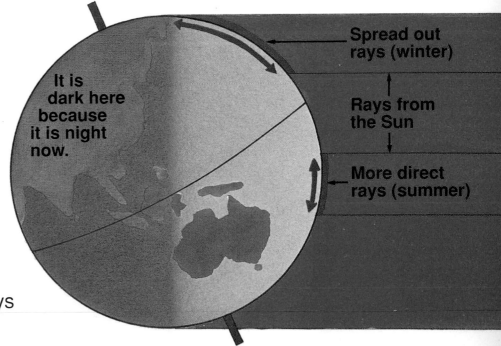

It is dark here because it is night now.

Spread out rays (winter)

Rays from the Sun

More direct rays (summer)

Weather power

Pollution from power stations, factories and cars is harming the world and the air we breathe. Using the Sun's heat and wind power does not cause pollution.

Wind power

You can make a windmill which lifts things when you blow at it and make it turn.

You need: paper, scissors, glue, 2 straws, model dough, paper clip, adhesive tape, thread, button.

1. Cut out a piece of paper about 10cm (4in) square, and cut slits as shown.

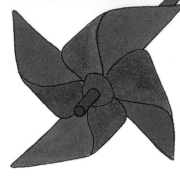

2. Fold the corners marked X into the middle. Glue them down.

3. Make a hole in the middle with a pencil. Push a straw through and squash model dough around it.

It looks like a windmill now.

4. Tape a paper clip to the second straw, like this. Push the windmill straw through the end of the paper clip.

Second straw

Windmill straw

5. Tape some thread to the windmill straw. Tie the button to the thread. Hold the second straw and blow at the windmill.

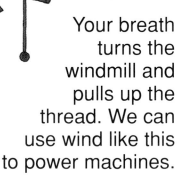

Your breath turns the windmill and pulls up the thread. We can use wind like this to power machines.

Solar water heating

Power from the Sun is called solar power. You can use the heat of the Sun on a summer day to heat water inside a garden hose.

Attach the hose to a tap and turn it on. Turn it off when water comes out of the other end. Stretch a balloon over the end.

The balloon keeps in the water.

Wind farms

In windy places, people are setting up wind farms. They are fields full of windmills which turn machinery to make electricity.

Stretch out the hose so that it is all lying in the sunshine.

After half an hour, take the balloon off the end and turn on the tap.

Sunny showers

In very sunny countries, many people have solar water heaters on their roofs. They warm water for baths and showers.

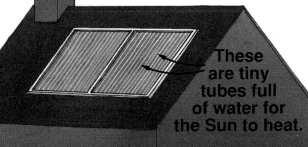

These are tiny tubes full of water for the Sun to heat.

The water that comes out first will be hotter than before, until more cold water from the tap comes through. The Sun has heated the water in the hose.

Notes for parents and teachers

These notes will help answer questions that may arise from the activities on earlier pages.

Water in the air (pages 52-53)

Like all substances, water is made up of tiny particles called molecules. They are constantly moving, and often break away and escape. This is called evaporation. Heating water gives the molecules more energy, so they can move around more easily.

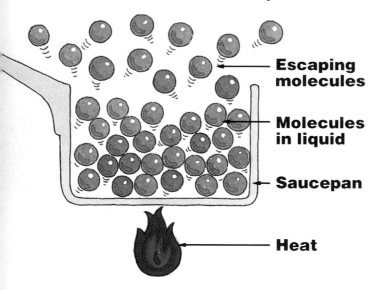

Escaping molecules

Molecules in liquid

Saucepan

Heat

Cooling the molecules makes them move more slowly. This enables them to condense and form a liquid again.

Clouds and rain (pages 54-55)

Although lots of rain comes from the sea, it is never salty. When water evaporates, it leaves behind things that are dissolved in it, like salt.

Cold weather (pages 56-57)

Cooling a liquid takes energy away from its molecules until they cannot break free. Each molecule is held in roughly the same position. This is when the liquid becomes a solid (freezes). Most liquids grow smaller as they freeze, but water takes up more space, because of the structure of its molecules.

It is possible for the sea to freeze. This usually only happens in polar regions, where it is extremely cold in the winter. It is much more difficult to make the sea freeze because it is salty. Salt water has a lower freezing point than fresh water.

All snowflakes are formed in the same way. Their patterns are made by the way the snowflakes vibrate as they fall through the air. This is why each one is unique.

Heating up (pages 64-65)

Pollution from factories, power stations and cars has increased the amount of carbon dioxide in the atmosphere. This is enhancing the greenhouse effect so the atmosphere traps more heat, and the temperature of the Earth rises. Scientists think this will change the world's climate, so people should try to prevent further pollution.

0° Celsius (32° Fahrenheit) is the freezing point of pure water.

Temperature is usually measured in degrees Celsius (centigrade) or degrees Fahrenheit. The temperatures given in weather forecasts are measurements taken in the shade.

Sun and shadows (66-67)

The way the Earth tilts means that there are three different weather patterns, or climates. The Arctic and Antarctic have polar climates. The areas between them and the Tropics of Cancer and Capricorn are temperate zones. Places between the Tropics have a tropical climate.

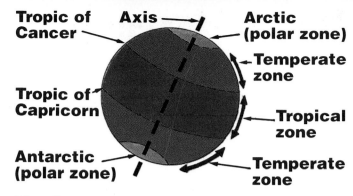

The Sun's rays always slant over the pole which is in daylight, so the weather there is always colder than in other areas. Temperate zones have four seasons when the weather is warmer or colder. The tropical areas are warm all year, as the Sun's light hits them very directly.

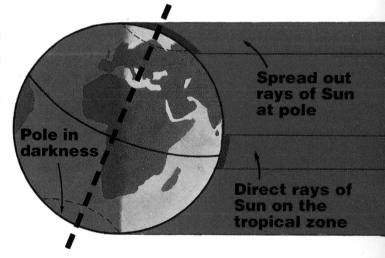

When one pole is in daylight, it is dark at the other. Each pole has six months of light, then six months of darkness.

71

Weather facts

Here are some incredible things you may not know about weather.

Hailstones are usually about the size of small peas. The biggest recorded hailstone was as big as a melon.

The weather helps spread the Sun's heat all over the Earth. Without weather, the poles would get so cold and the Equator so hot that nothing could live on the Earth.

There have been many reports of rains of fish or frogs. Tornadoes may have sucked them up and dropped them later as "rain".

The wettest place in the world is Mount Wai-'ale-'ale in Hawaii. It gets about 335 days of rain a year.

In Europe, the winters between about 1400 and 1850 were very cold. The River Thames in London froze over. Fairs were sometimes held on the ice, which was so thick that an elephant could have walked on it.

Tornadoes suck up things in their path. One plucked all the feathers off some chickens. Somehow, the chickens survived.

Index

Answers to puzzles

Page 5 – Touch the wires to corners C and D to complete the circuit and light the bulb.

Page 38 – Another joint that bends like your elbow is your knee.

First published in 1992 by Usborne Publishing Ltd, Usborne House, 83-85 Saffron Hill, London EC1N 8RT, England. www.usborne.com